Weather Watchers

Snow

Cassie Mayer

Heinemann Library
Chicago, Illinois

Photo research by Tracy Cummins, Tracey Engel, and Ruth Blair
Designed by Jo Hinton-Malivoire
Printed and bound in China by South China Printing Company

10 09 08 07 06
10 9 8 7 6 5 4 3 2 1

Library of Congress Cataloging-in-Publication Data
Mayer, Cassie.
  Snow / Cassie Mayer.-- 1st ed.
      p. cm. -- (Weather watchers)
  Includes bibliographical references and index.
  ISBN-13: 978-1-4034-8415-4 (library binding-hardcover : alk. paper)
  ISBN-10: 1-4034-8415-5 (library binding-hardcover : alk. paper)
  ISBN-13: 978-1-4034-8423-9 (pbk. : alk. paper)
  ISBN-10 1-4034-8423-6 (pbk. : alk. paper)
 1. Snow--Juvenile literature. I. Title. II. Series.
  QC926.37.M39 2007
  551.57'84--dc22
                              2006007905

Acknowledgments
The author and publisher are grateful to the following for permission to reproduce copyright material:
Corbis pp. **4** (cloud; sunshine, G. Schuster/zefa; rain, Anthony Redpath), **7** (Matthias Kulka), **8** (Craig Tuttle), **15** (Jonathan Blair), **16** (Grafton Marshall Smith), **17** (David Pollack), **20** (Darrell Gulin), **23** (snowflake, Matthias Kulka; blizzard, Grafton Marshall Smith); Getty Images pp. **4** (lightning; snow, Marc Wilson Photography), **5** (Marc Wilson Photography), **6** (Chris Hackett), **9** (Kennan Harvey), **14** (Yuri Dojc), **19** (Michael Dunning), **21** (Brian Bailey), **23** (water vapor, Kennan Harvey); Photo Researchers, Inc. p. **18** (B. & C. Alexander).

Cover photograph reproduced with permission of Getty Images (Stone/Christoph Burki).
Back cover photograph reproduced with permission of Getty Images (Brian Bailey).

Every effort has been made to contact copyright holders of any material reproduced in this book. Any omissions will be rectified in subsequent printings if notice is given to the publisher.

Contents

What Is Weather?

Weather is what the air is like outside.
Weather can change all the time.

Snow is a type of weather.

What Is Snow?

Snow falls from clouds.
Snow falls when it is cold.

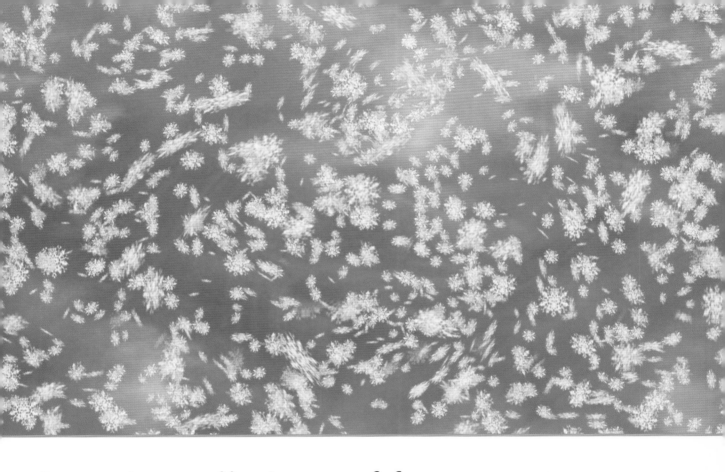

Snow is small pieces of frozen water.
These pieces are called snowflakes.

water vapor

Snowflakes are made from water vapor.
Water vapor comes from oceans.

water vapor

Water vapor comes from living things.

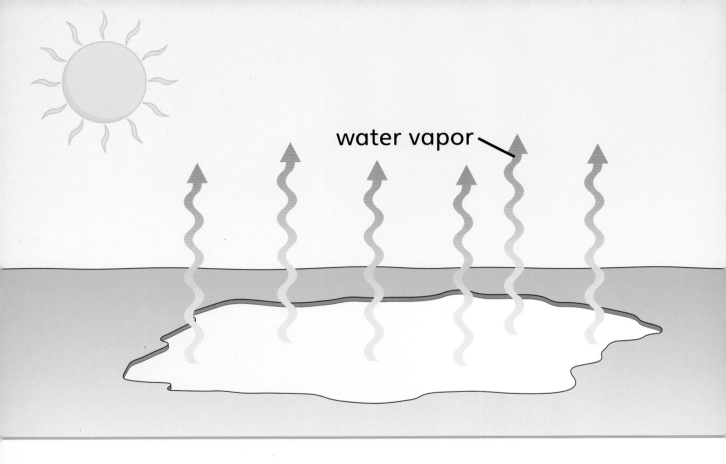

water vapor

Water vapor rises into the air.

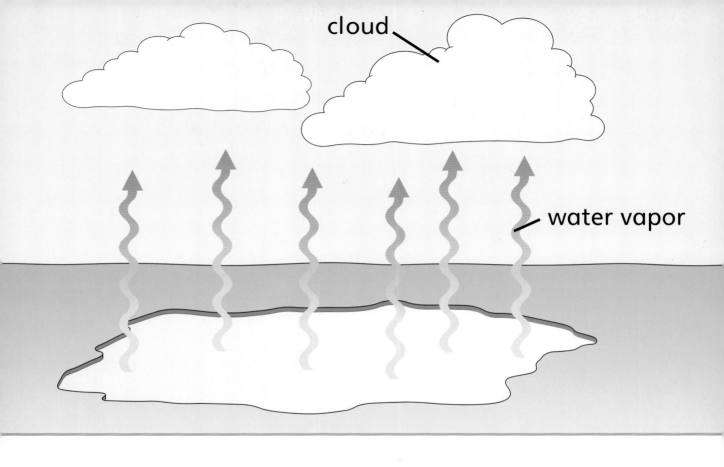

cloud

water vapor

Water vapor forms clouds.

frozen water vapor

Water vapor freezes in the cloud.

snowflake

Then water vapor forms snowflakes.
Big snowflakes fall from the cloud.

Types of Snow

Heavy snow falls when it is not too cold.
Heavy snow sticks together.

Light snow falls when it is very cold.
Light snow does not stick together.

Sometimes it snows a lot.
This is called a blizzard.

Blizzards have strong winds.
Blizzards can be unsafe.

Snow Around the World

Some places get a lot of snow.

Some places get no snow.

How Does Snow Help Us?

Living things need water to grow.
Snow brings water back to the earth.

Snow is an important part of our weather. Snow is also fun!

What to Wear When It Snows

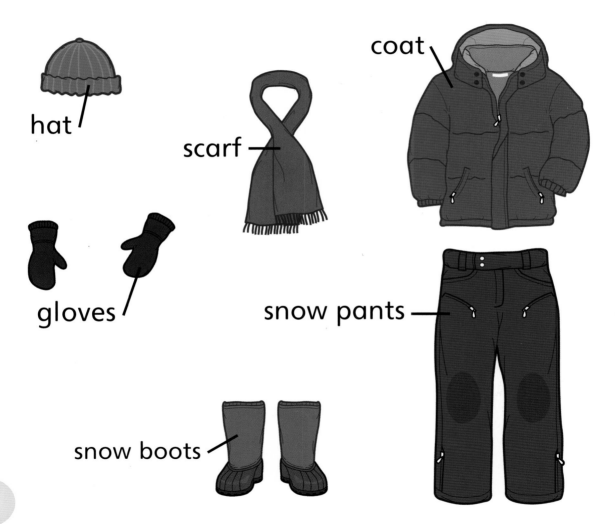

hat

scarf

coat

gloves

snow pants

snow boots

Picture Glossary

 **blizzard** a big snowstorm with strong winds

 **snowflake** a tiny piece of frozen water. Snowflakes fall from clouds.

 **water vapor** part of the air outside

Index

Note to Parents and Teachers
This series introduces children to the concept of weather and its importance in our lives. Discuss with children the types of weather that they are already familiar with, and point out how weather changes season by season.

In this book, children explore snow. Diagrams are included to enhance students' understanding of how snow is formed. The text has been chosen with the advice of a literacy expert to enable beginning readers success reading independently or with moderate support. An expert in the field of meteorology was consulted to ensure accurate content. You can support children's nonfiction literacy skills by helping them use the table of contents, headings, picture glossary, and index.